THE SIEGE

Written by Elizabeth McCabe
Illustrated by Mike Johnson

ETA®
Cuisenaire

The Seige
ISBN 0-7406-1016-3
ETA 351111

Revised American edition published in 2004 by ETA/Cuisenaire®
under license from Era Publications. All rights reserved.

ETA/Cuisenaire Product Development Manager: Mary Watanabe
Lead Editor: Betty Hey
Editorial Team: Kevin Anderson, Kim O'Brien, Nancy Sheldon,
  Elizabeth Sycamore
Educational Consultant: Geraldine Haggard, Ed.D.

ETA/Cuisenaire • Vernon Hills, IL 60061-1862
800-445-5985 • www.etacuisenaire.com

Printed in China.

04 05 06 07 08 09 10 11 12 13   10 9 8 7 6 5 4 3 2 1

THE SIEGE

A thief stole all the chocolate in the world. The people could not imagine life without chocolate, but how could they get it back?

A wise mother helps the people figure out a clever plan.

Elizabeth McCabe's funny story and Mike Johnson's hilarious illustrations will keep you laughing all the way to the surprise ending.

Once there was a thief who stole all the chocolate in the world. He took it to a castle on top of a cliff.

He went to the top of the castle and called out, "If you want it, come and get it. Har-har-har-har!"

"How can we get the chocolate back?" said the people. "It is in a castle. The castle is big. The castle is strong. The doors are locked. The windows have bars. There are guards on the inside and guards on the outside. It's impossible!"

"It does look impossible," said
a little girl. "But my mother
says *nothing's* impossible."

"She does?" said the people.
"Then let's go and ask her
what to do."

So the people went to the little girl's mother. They said, "A thief has stolen all the chocolate. We can't get it back. He has put it in a castle. The castle is big.

The castle is strong. The doors are locked. The windows have bars. There are guards on the inside and guards on the outside. It's impossible!"

"Nothing's impossible," said
Frances (which was the name
of the little girl's mother).

"But why do you want it back? After all, it's only chocolate!"

"Only chocolate?" said the people.

"Only *chocolate*!

"Only …
chocolate pudding,
chocolate candy,
chocolate cookies,
chocolate peanuts,
chocolate syrup,
chocolate cake …
we can't live without
chocolate!"

"If you can't live without chocolate," said Frances, "you must go to the castle and get it back."

"But the castle is big.
The castle is …"

"I know all that," said Frances, "but there is a way. Take this box. It's an *idea* box.

Put it in the middle of town.
Tell everyone who has an idea
to put it in here.

"Then try all of the ideas. One of them will get the chocolate back. But I can't see why you're bothering at all!"

After one week, the people
came to see what ideas
had been put in the box.

Idea 1 —
Try hooks and crooks.
Idea 2 —
Try towers and showers.

Idea 3 —
Try trees and bees.
Idea 4 —
Try doctors and 'copters.

Every idea seemed
like a good one. So
they tried them all.

But the castle was big. The castle was strong. The doors were locked. The windows had bars. There were guards on the inside and guards on the outside. It was impossible!

"We'll have to give up!" said the people.

"Wait!" said the mayor. "There's one more idea."

"Let's see," said the people.
"It says,

> Let no fruit, no vegetables,
> no toothbrushes, no
> toothpaste, and especially
> no dentists into the castle.

"Let's try it!"

So the people stopped
all fruit,
all vegetables,
all toothbrushes,
and toothpaste
from going into the castle.

And they stopped dentists from getting in as well.

At first nothing happened.

But then, one by one, guards with bandages around their jaws came out of the castle to give themselves up.

And at last the thief gave himself up, too.

"I never want to see another bar of chocolate as long as I live," he said.

Of course, the people had
a gigantic Chocolate Party
to celebrate their victory.

But they were careful not to eat too much. After all, the dentists in town were far too busy to see *them*.

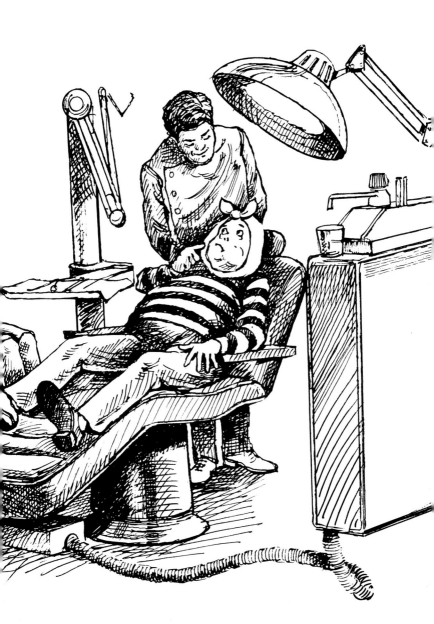